ART NOUVEAU

COLORING BOOK

— • • • —

BIRD DESIGNS

Art Mill aims to satisfy your exquisite taste and nourish your creativity with the best art books on the market!

ART NOUVEAU SERIES BY ART MILL

30 sensual hand drawn Bird designs, all inspired by the masters of Art Nouveau such as Alphonse Mucha, William Morris, Anton Seder and many more.

FIVE BONUS DESIGNS ARE INCLUDED
JUST IN CASE YOU WOULD LIKE TO HAVE A SECOND GO!

ESCAPE TO A WORLD OF INSPIRATION AND RELAXATION
WITH OTHER BOOKS IN THE SERIES:

MYSTERIOUS SEA LIFE	GLORIOUS FLOWERS	FASCINATING INSECTS	PLANT AND ANIMAL DESIGNS

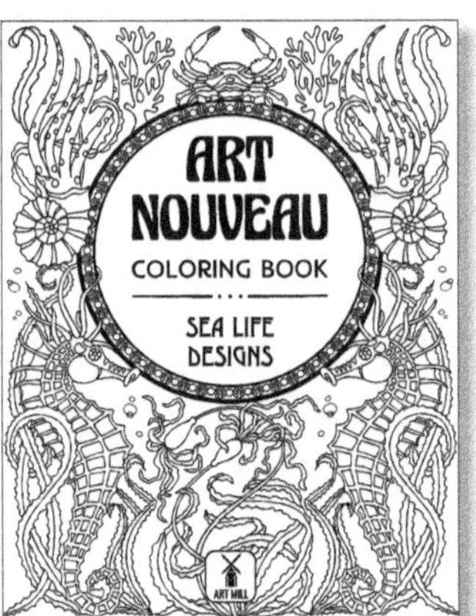
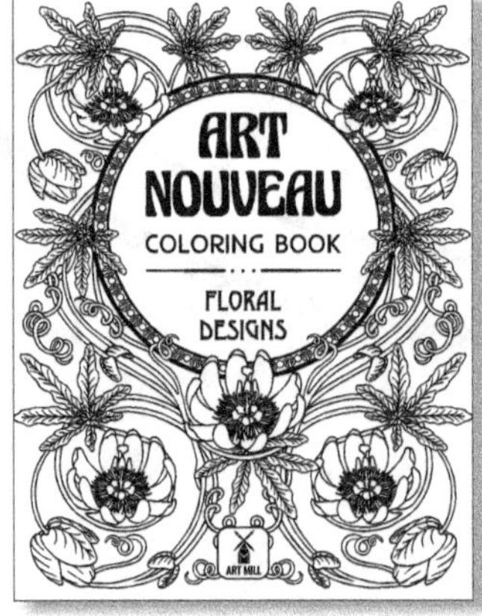
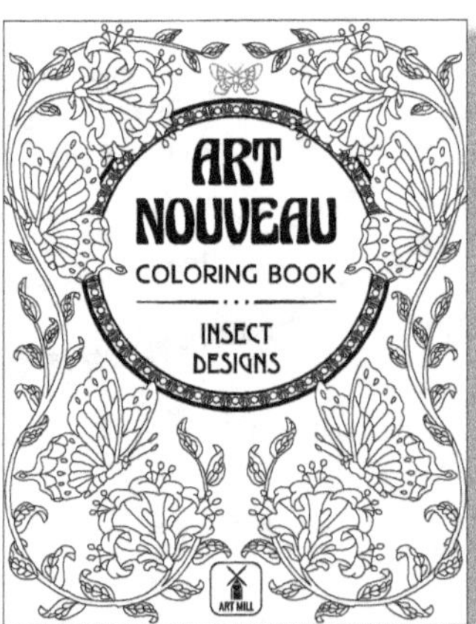
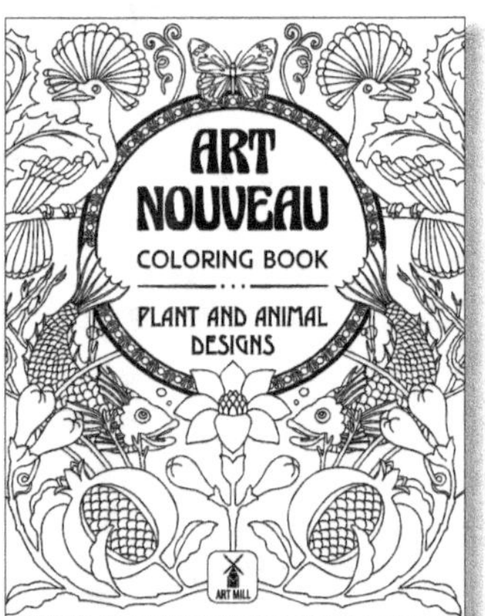

Join us on social media for some inspiration and updates!

- Art Mill Books
- artmillbooks
- E-mail: artmillbooks@gmail.com

FEEL FREE TO GIVE US AN HONEST REVIEW AND ANY FEEDBACK ON AMAZON!

BONUS
PAGES
Have
a
Second go!
ART MILL